Other Titles by Richard Harrison

Big Breath of a Wish
Fathers Never Leave You
Hero of the Play
Now is the Winter: Thinking about Hockey (edited with Jamie Dopp)
On Not Losing My Father's Ashes in the Flood
Recovering the Naked Man
Secret Identity Reader: Essays on Sex, Death and the Superhero (with Lee Easton)
Worthy of His Fall

Cover image: Jared Shapiro
Cover and interior design: Jared Shapiro
Author photograph: Lisa Rouleau
Typeset in Crimson Text and Blockletter
Printed by Coach House Printing Company Toronto, Canada

10 9 8 7 6 5 4 3 2 1

The publisher gratefully acknowledges the support of the Ontario Arts
Council, the Canada Council for the Arts and the Government of Canada.

Wolsak and Wynn Publishers, Ltd.
280 James Street North
Hamilton, ON
Canada L8R 2L3

Library and Archives Canada Cataloguing in Publication

Title: 25 : hockey poems, new and revised / Richard Harrison.
Other titles: Poems. Selections (Wolsak and Wynn Publishers) | Hockey
    poems, new and revised | Twenty-five
Names: Harrison, Richard, 1957- author.
Description: Includes revised poems previously published in Hero of
    the play.
Identifiers: Canadiana 20190159758 | ISBN 9781989496060 (softcover)
Subjects: LCSH: Hockey—Poetry.
Classification: LCC PS8565.A6573 A6 2019 | DDC C811/.54—dc23

● For Lisa

CONTENTS

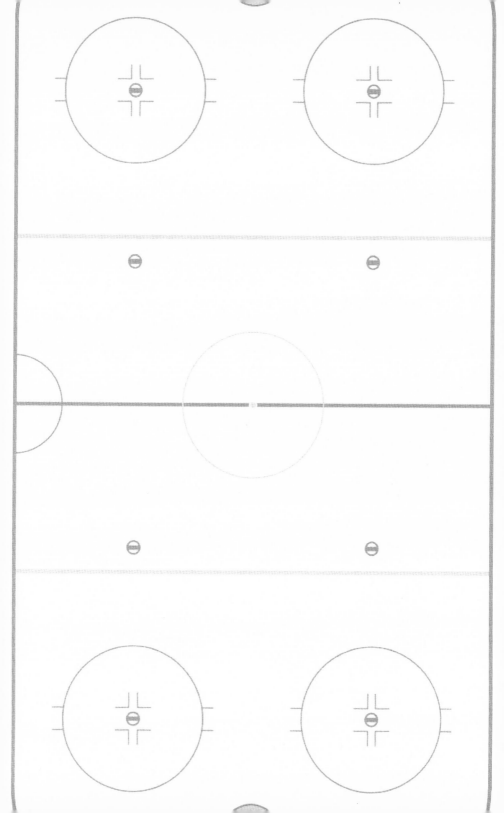

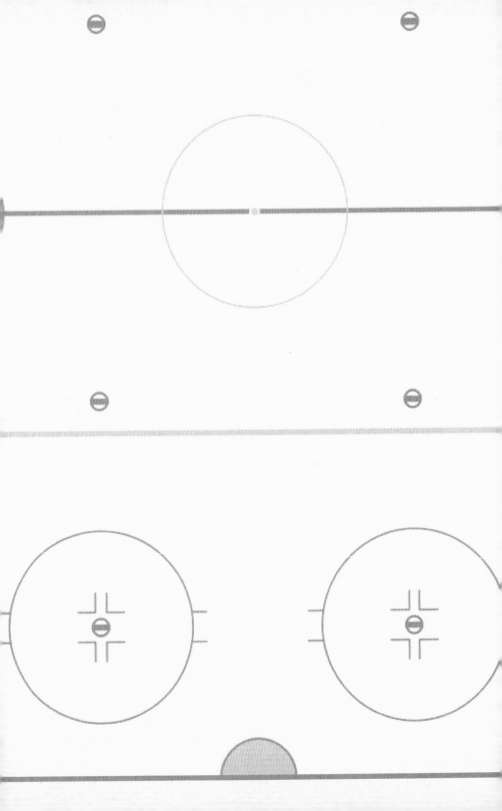

INTRODUCTION

This book got its start with a poem that began,

> Taking a small picture of myself, I cut out my face,
> paste it over Brett Hull's face in a photo of him
> and Bobby at some charity hockey game in
> Duluth. I send you this as further proof that I
> played with Bobby in '76 when I was scouted
> by the Jets for goal.

This was 1989, and I was at play: with heroes, with fathers and sons, the mythology of the game and with the language of hockey, which is intimately connected to the Canadian vocabulary as a whole. I enjoyed what I'd made. I thought there might be a suite of poems there.

Then I went travelling, and in Abidjan on the Ivory Coast I encountered the rink that did triple duty for figure skating, curling and hockey in the Hôtel Ivoire. Hockey had arrived before me. I skated on that rink, and the words of the game had meaning in a place I'd never imagined the game could be experienced. I felt a new love there for hockey the way you feel love for your home when some part of it you left behind surprises you in a foreign land. There was more to write.

A few people thought that hockey would be the last thing I either would, or should, write about at the time. I was one of them, too, despite all that attracted me to the work. Marja Jacobs, then one of the publishers at Wolsak & Wynn to whom I showed an early manuscript, remembers me as shy about it. Hockey didn't fit with the poems I had written before, attending to the sensitivities of our lives, and to all the social ills that work against all that's vulnerable in us. Hockey, loud hockey in the image of the NHL with its fraternal brutality and commercialism and celebration of power and our joy in its display, ran counter to the politic with which I had defined myself and my poetry.

But even though appreciating sport is different from appreciating art, it's a false difference if it's thought of as a mutually exclusive one. I've known all my life that the athlete and the poet have much in common. My father was a sportsman and a soldier, and those two parts of him were irreversibly joined. He had his finest athletic moments on the track during the games the British Army held for the troops in Southeast Asia. He was also, as I tell everyone, deeply in love with the poetry he memorized both in his school days and after. The recitations of poetry that came from the voice within that athletic body of his, with its strength and aggression, and the timing of a great throw, those recitations made loving the poet in him and the athlete in him all of a piece.

In the hockey players whom I've met because of *Hero of the Play* – Maurice Richard, Bobby Hull, Jean Béliveau, Gordie Howe, Tiger Williams, the list goes on – I have found that same love of both the body in action and the words that raise themselves to art describing it. For all of those players, the poems about their sport gave them back something of their own vision of its meaning. With each of them, I was able to talk without the wall between fan and hero, not as if I, too, had played, but because the poems knew the game as one who had.

Over the years, this became true for more than just those players who could see themselves in the poems because they were there by name. I have seen it in high school students – usually, but not always, young men – who generally played on their school teams, and who perked up to listen to "Stanley Cup": "At the centre of the circle of the champions of the world / Mario Lemieux hoists the Cup." For them poetry class was least of their learning because poetry showed them little or nothing of their own lives. But this poem and its fellows showed that poetry, as the first poets taught, is language that, if it is successful, immortalizes, and if it is not, still says that what it speaks of should not disappear. Athletes respect that, and I think it's because athletes respect words even more than poets do. Poets always have more. There's always another page, but for a kid on the bench, there is no more powerful poem than when the coach stands beside them and says, "You're not playing tonight."

Hockey is a game of speech. Listen to both teammates and opponents talking to each other as the game progresses. Listen to the commentators on TV, or the broadcasters on radio, creating a story out of the swirl and clash of players before them. Even without seeing Henderson's goal in game eight in Russia, we can feel its excitement in Foster Hewitt's crackling gramophone voice declaring, "Henderson has scored for Canada!" – one of the greatest moments in our national play-by-play. And listen to fans talking, creating worlds of hockey talk – analysis, jokes, puns, historical references, wordplay.

That is the foundation of the poem, the love of language not for what it's telling, but for the play of it, how it joins us in that play. That is what I found myself on the edge of entering in the late 1980s and early '90s when I was beginning what I knew by then would have to be a book. I had used hockey metaphors in a few poems. I had written about a few hockey stories and built them, as you do with fantasies, around the real-life connections and conflicts to which they leant a rich imagery. Hockey may be life for some, but for most of us it is a source of occasional and vivid metaphors.

So I went in, determined to test the language of hockey. It was built for the game, but it applied beyond it. Could I get *everything* into it? Everything about which I wanted to write? The answer was no. But my attempt found its limit after going much farther into my own life and the experiences of others than I ever thought it would. I did have the idea at one point that my hockey book would be the one at the greatest distance from me. If sport was an escape, writing about it could be, too. It's an easy mistake, and one I'm happiest now, twenty-five years after *Hero,* to have realized I didn't make. As my friends – thank you, Noelle Allen, Jamie Dopp, Paul Martin and especially Lisa Rouleau, among others – have shown me over the years, the hockey poems have drawn from my life – and worked their way back into it – as much as any poems I've written. I didn't know it. At the time, I was focusing on each poem the way you focus on the handful of seconds in a play that you actually have the puck. But that, too, is a portrait of the poet as athlete, the athlete as artist: you don't know the meaning of the game as a whole until you've played to the end. Then you open the book you've made one poem at a time, and there it is.

Richard Harrison, June 2019

RESTING PLACES

In memory of fighting men Bob Probert and Ralph Harrison

Bob Probert's brother poured Bob's ashes
          into the penalty box at Joe Louis arena,
the perfect resting place
                    because Bob did a lot of time there
          for pummelling men so thoroughly,
                         they became afraid of hockey.

And a former student of mine,
          drafted by the Bruins in the late '80s,
when he came back from winter camp, he said,

          I fought Probert! *Want to know how?*
                    I pulled his sweater down like this,
                         held his arms –
                              and yelled Ref!!

There they go,
          slow dancing down the ice:
gigantic Bob knowing the slick plays he made in junior
          would never earn him a spot
               in the hockey lore,
                    or the All-Star Game,
          or protecting the captain on Detroit's top line;

and my student knowing he'd never make pro.

Bob died the way a lot of enforcers die –
          cells falling lights out into his brain
               like grains of dust filling a music box.

Still, his brother gave his ashes to the rink.

          We love best the circles we complete.

In a few months,
        I will go to Oxford and
                read from a book with my father in the title.

I will take a small jar of his ashes
        to leave behind because years ago,

when I was in the running
        for a place at the most sacred school
                in the Empire of my father's army,

he looked at me like he'd won the war,
        and said,

                Oxford! –

the old fighter still in awe of
        the citadel he'd defended, standing now,
                full of doors,

                none of which opened for him.

THE GREATS

These are the figures of my escape: men who could
fly, bend steel, come to life each month in my eager
eyes, my flight from my father's face. Determined men
I watch cross and recross the comic-panel lines that
mark their play; these are my figures, the Greats.
A sheet of ice puts a man in motion at impossible
angles for the physics of the shoe; an ink-filled brush
over thick paper . . . *I can move like you.*

MY FAVOURITES (THE NATIONAL GAME)

This one from the summer of '88 when I picked up
the habit of cards and my father called from Victoria,
collecting with me . . . *I've got Bobby Hull,* his voice soft,
proud, my father at his best. It's Bobby at his peak as
a Black Hawk rounding the boards in his own end with
the puck for another breakneck rush up ice. Then
this one of Bobby as a Jet – after the divorce, the time
he says he lost his hair before the world. Here his scalp
is stitched through with brass and goals no one counts
except in brackets. This one – Luc Robitaille, *Best
left-winger ever born in Quebec.* Marc gave him to me hidden
in a bowl of popcorn, tattered and folded the way
teenagers love and reject the selfsame thing. And
this one you sent me in the mail because you lived
in Regina and I lived here. Brett Hull, poised, intent,
waiting for the pass.

REUNION, OR GRIEVING

Taking a small picture of myself, I cut out my face
and paste it over Brett Hull's face in a photo of him
and Bobby at some charity hockey game in Duluth.
I send you this as further proof that I practiced
with Bobby in '76 when I was scouted by the Jets
for goal. Bobby is proud of his son, the pride
coming only now into the light of the arena where
they are perfectly again husband and child together.
Many will say this is cheap, ask where was he when
Brett was growing up waiting for Bobby to appear
in the almost-empty stands of junior. Today I got
the news: months ago my place was vacant
at my stepson's wedding. *How could you?* the face
beneath my face moves my mouth and asks me.

WHY THE PETERBOROUGH PETES WON THE MEMORIAL CUP

It was the first time
we undressed for each other,
and when she took off her shirt,
and I pulled off mine,
I heard music
and cheering
from far away.
She undid her bra,
and we both
heard it then.
The noise got louder
as we took off our jeans,
and louder still
as she slid off her panties.
By now we were both naked
and laughing
on our side
of the front door,
and the cars rolled by
and the band played
and the drummers
drummed like hearts.
As we held each other,
the fans cheered,
Go! Petes! Go!
And the city celebrated
the triumph of its team,
while we kissed each other
all over,
we kissed each other
all over
our lips in a revel
everywhere we kissed.

LOVE AND THE HOCKEY POOL

1. Draft Day

Among the ten of us who sit together and draft
players by name, I know only Robert because once
you and he were lovers. Now you are friends: there
it is. I want it to be as if we had known each other
from the days of table hockey when each of us was
complete and right with himself as instinct. When the
games begin, my pick Bourque goes down with a
shoulder, and Ricci, my horse for Rookie of the Year,
the kid from my adopted hometown junior team, he
breaks a hand trying to grab a slapshot. Robert calls
me up and leaves a message: *Your team SUCKS!* he
says, and laughs, and we become close. But when
Messier, his main man, falls to the ice and cannot rise
without his teammates' help, the iron box of his face
unhinged, *oh no oh no* going through his mind, his leg
curled like a baby's, I feel no *there but for the grace,*
only the gain of my own leg on the scoresheet. Now
we are closer.

2. Ice

About the surface. Counting. Hard-edged things.
Like ice and pennies; in the face-off circle, a skate
cuts *R loves L, R loves L.* The beginning of the story
is the theory of jealousy, the game about every-
thing except the goals and assists, the colourful,
public men we pass between us, your name un-
spoken. This is the meaning of victory – a puck
sliding over ice into the bag of cords that holds a
man to his duty – that I should be the one, the
winner, how I come to love him, hate him, the
mirror your love brings me to face.

THE PRAISE OF MEN

To their faces, it escapes me, words for the praise of men.
To a man I admire, to whom I would say, You have real
talent and my envy, all that comes out is, *You're good,*
and there I remain, fatherly, in charge of words by *not*
saying them. Give me these players whom I will never
meet to hoot and holler out my deepest riskless love that
finds no softer words, no shame or venture, merely
a game, the bargain sealed with a seat in the blues,
my naked face a dab of camouflage, hiding my praise
in the open.

AFRICAN HOCKEY POEMS

1. Pre-Game Skate

When the manager of the gallery in the Hôtel
Ivoire sees the flag on my pack, he tells me he
loves my country, and he plays hockey on the rink
that lies chilled like a pie in the middle of the hotel
on the equator where leaves rot as they grow and
the air is sweet as apples with their dying. I say
What position? He says, *Left wing.* I say, *Like
Bobby Hull.* And Bobby's name makes it: he draws
his hand up, and it smiles at the end of his arm:
this is the Shake, the one that begins with the slap
of palm against palm, the one between men
who've found enough between them to confirm
the world for a day and go on. Tomorrow I will
skate on this rink like the pros back home, way
ahead of schedule and nature; I will tell you
I touched the ice and I could be any boy in love.

2. Road Trip

For the photo shoot in the only rink in the Côte
d'Ivoire, I carry a hockey stick from the Canadian
Embassy into the streets of Abidjan, and the stares
of the passersby say no one knows what it is just as
the inland farmers who had never seen the sea stared
at Ulysses with his oar. The old king waited for those
stares, the oar become a butter churn, a plough,
the village speaker's staff; when the business of the
day gives way to night, it is time for the story to be told.

3. Play-By-Play

This is hockey where it has never been written: an
ordinary stick on an African street, my hand on the
shaft, my foot stubbing the butt. I'm walking the way
I walked as a child in the old world of Tony and
Chris and Russell and me playing the sun below the
level of the street. You couldn't see the ball until it hit.
In Hull's hands it was a million-dollar shot, the birth
of the mask, thousands in the stands waiting for
the stick to go up and back and BOOM! – *I know!*
calls a man, and he takes the stick from me, waggles
his head from side to side – *shusshh, shusshh*, he says
as surely as I do, raised on the sound effects of ice.

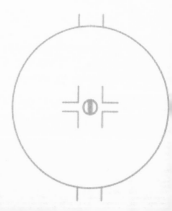

HOCKEY MOM

For Joan Shillington

Your son amazes with this stomach. *I swear,* you say,
he was born eating steak and eggs for breakfast.
And when he comes home from practice at midnight,
it's *Mom, can you fix me a plate?* At the rink, though,
you tell me, you turn away and walk down stone
into the smell of shaved ice melting and every fabric
sweat can soak. He's out there on his frozen planet,
hurling the body you've fed every day of his life
and then some, and, sure, there are Spartan mothers
in the stands screaming any one of murder's names
as if a woman's voice could arm her boy for the work
of wood and bone the men and audience all think is
part of the game forever. So he skates and takes his hits.
And you return to your seat with nothing but your breath
to hold, and you watch his hungry body disappear with
every bite and healing muscle into the player you surprise
yourself dreaming with him he'll be.

RUSSIANS

We need them. They made the act of a single Canadian
Canada's act in '72, the shot so sweet it has replayed
a million times: Henderson, leaping, faces the camera as if
it's each of us; Cournoyer embraces his ribs, CANADA
on his shoulders. And the Soviets, confused, upset,
they left him uncovered and Canada's greatest shot
was a rebound; I tell you how good it felt to win, and
you, trying to love me in this moment, ask, *Who's this?*
Tretiak, their goalie a crab on its back every limb
kicking out to stop what's already been done. *And this?*
Number 25 on the Russian defence – *I don't know,*
his name unwritten below the painting of this photograph
in the Hall of Fame, and on the back of the Summit
Series Anniversary card where he takes up a quarter of
the frame and already he understands what they've lost.
They played the better game and should have beaten
the high-priced men who laughed at their ancient skates
and the way their trainer collected the pucks in a plastic
bucket during practice because they had so few. He sees
himself as a promising child; he made older boys look
clumsy in their parents' eyes, the words *National Team*
were said in his presence and he never saw those boys
again; he sees his country's junior team humbling
yet another nation on its home ice, the fans sullen and
quiet in the stands. He sees the young man whose leg was
broken during tryouts and never healed right. They turn
to face him. Player by player, he sees the death of his league,
and at the other end of the arena, he sees Phil Esposito
with his own team in the NHL take the podium on draft
day, and with all the world to choose from, pluck a kid
from Europe happy to make it on the only rinks that count.
He did his best. They almost won. His own name forgotten,
he is looking where you are, and you are asking me,
Find him.

MALE BONDING

Once I loved other sons as though I found my
brother again: the years of their growing muscles
and tanned skin, the evening excursions to the
arcades downtown where our faces were reflected
in the games, the way someone standing in the living
room is on TV when it is off. I thought I could never
leave. The traded player says, *I cannot go, I belong
here on the shared ice.* These are the men I've
learned to skate with, take a pass, shoot, share the
jubilance of the goal. But he goes, and he puts on
another uniform, and he loves his old team from
a great distance, loving like men around their loss.

HIS FATHER'S NUMBER

John Cullen on Gardens' ice with his father's
number, better than the flag to wrap an admiring
son, his father in the stands like a patriot, father of
numbers. And the father glows on the son's back in
the light of the stadium; this is hockey's most
treasured story: men grow old under their numbers
which are their names from the lofty seats, and the
day their names come again. In my father's flesh
are memories of the body become manly and
skilled; there is always the test of *true to yourself,*
and a man can see his answer in the way his body
cuts through a chilling air, stretches out his arms
into the sleeves of his father's shirt.

HRUDEY

Boxed in by the mask, the goalie is the one whose face we invent from his style. Not just *stand-up* or *butterfly*, but *the one who talks to the posts,* or *the one who leans on his stick in meditation.* With Hrudey it was the pale ribbons that hung from the back of his helmet. My brother and I called him *The Samurai* when he wielded the blade for New York. But when he stood with the Kings in the heart of the silence of Montreal in December '89, I saw them for the sign white ribbons would later become – the world could be wrapped in grief and still hold on to hope. Now, boxed in by TV, he appears, all face, in my living room. When the game is slowed by videotape, he lets me get what he had to catch full speed. And he laughs a lot more than I would ever have guessed.

A MID-ICE PROPOSAL

For Irwin, and for Amy & Ty

My friend Irwin sends me a photograph and a suggestion:
You should write about this. In the photo, at centre ice after
a game, a man is asking his girlfriend to marry him. Both
teams are there, too, standing in a ring, the man on his knee,
which is trickier than you think on skates, even if staying
upright is the only thing in the balance. They're all in their
gear, and the wet, good smell of play is on them. Even the
Zamboni is there, started up but parked behind, so that in
the photograph its flank could be the wall of the home
where they'll one day live. *Write about this because this is about
hockey,* my friend says. Yes. Hockey. Hockey is here. Hockey
is everywhere in this country. At the folk festival last
weekend, after the protest songs against George Bush's war,
hockey was the most popular topic. Stompin' Tom waited
until the end of his set to give us "The Hockey Song" we'd
waited for all night, then introduced "Hockey Mom" –
a tune to correct the lack of a hero yet unsung. Before him,
the homer from Philadelphia raised his voice in epic melody
to praise Dave Schultz, whose fans came to their seats
wearing the German helmets from WW II, and charged the
boards with their iron heads when the Hammer beat down
some scofflaw who got what he deserved in the fearsome
system of Flyer justice in its day. You see? All the great
questions are covered by hockey – birth and death, life and
song, and here, hope and love on a beer-league rink in BC,
in that Delphic circle where length and breadth intersect
and the puck's first fall defines the game.

BECAUSE THEY MAKE DECISIONS WHILE MOVING

Because they make decisions while moving, they are
not stunned by the terrible moment the puck hits
the stick, the skaters swirling like oil; in that moment,
they are perfect and faster than the speed of our
judgment. Only later does a man weep for his dead
father who believed for so long in his son. Only later
does it return to mind that management has cheated
him, or tomorrow he might be traded, or injured, or
wake in a city he does not love without a father to
call in the middle of his night, or somehow it might
leave him, what he is, just before he glances up and
shoots.

RICCI

In your first game for Philadelphia you, a centre,
reached out at your own blue line and tried to catch a
slapshot. You broke your hand, lost your chance at
Rookie of the Year; where you played junior I made
a stepfamily. You woke up this morning traded, the
clock at zero; the bones in your hand ache. At my
wedding there will be no stepsons, -daughter; there
will be Lisa and me, and this time I will give my
whole body, even the bones that once were broken.

WITHOUT WORDS

In October 1992, Calgary centre Joe Nieuwendyk
was elbowed in the throat and suffered an injury to his larynx.
At the time it was feared he'd never speak again.

I speak as a shell speaks, remembering in the cavern of
its heart the roaring ocean that tossed it up to a human
hand. Turn your face from the Saddledome on a
Saturday night. There I am pure action, and innocent as
hockey itself when winter stuns the mouth of the river
and metal chafes ice into boys at play, the words only
half a language and loved for that. Like poetry. I ap-
proach. My whole body becomes the lump in my throat
as if his criminal elbow is still there, as if it will last
forever, as if the iced and wasted land ended with
a bang along the boards one night. But I have our
names within me, close my lips around the roughened
air, and the world begins again between us in a whisper.

WHAT IT TAKES

*For Bernie Federko on the occasion of his induction
into the Hockey Hall of Fame, November 2002*

Any Saskatchewan kid who lays his head
on the dark earth dreaming in a crown of brome
can find it in the sweater he brought to Foam Lake
trimmed the colours of the prairie sky in summer.
And the men who picked enough roots and stones
from their fathers' land to tell could see it when
they rested by the boards and watched him
practice on the rink – Don't forget the work.
Take the ice the way you enter a room. Learn
everyone by name. When you have the puck,
more often than not, the goal is another man away.
Give everything its place. When he was named
to the Hall of Fame, first thing Bernie did
was call his friends, and, in a voice still shocked
with unexpected joy, give away what
a thousand games of pro will teach a man who listens:
You do your best, he said, *but you never know.*

LEMIEUX, AND THE NEWS

is cancer, and the doctors assure us of his strength, the
high probability of health. We say all we care about is
him even if he never plays again though we want him
back on the ice as he was, victorious. The news is the
punishment of Iraq, a surgical strike, the language
confusing life with one of its parts and not by accident
either. Today my friend Bill lost his friend who wore
his white hair long as if the '60s meant his age,
quoted with a tongue full of English letters, disdained
sentiment and had a collection of shillings, he said,
because of their shape. And this, suddenly, after weeks
of chemo and a good prognosis. Bill visited him the day
before, the way I wish I had visited when I had the
chance: do the usual talk about a book, eat and drink
all evening, laugh at what they expect you to
believe night after night, saying *See you tomorrow* like
it was the most normal thing in the world.

THE SWEATER

Could I tell you he was beautiful, returned from
winter camp in a sweater really from the team whose
crest it bore, him standing among us with our hands
outstretched; I touched the cloth. Shall I tell you
of his smile, his reckless arms that day; in a hockey town
he was a son in his father's own colours, how the son
once called his favourite teacher *Coach* and the father,
meeting that teacher, took his thin, long hand in his
huge fingers, enfolding it in inescapable size and said,
My son loved *you!* Shall I speak of love then, too?
A black suit burning gold at the edge; in the middle
of class this young man held up his arm in a sleeve of
Stanley Cups.

STANLEY CUP

At the centre of the circle of the Champions of the
World, Mario Lemieux hoists the Cup, kisses its silver
thigh, the names of men where *his* will soon be cut
with a finish pure as a mirror; around him, the
tumult. And Scotty Bowman, the winningest coach
in the NHL, named his second son Stanley when his
Canadiens won it in '73 with a stonewall blue line and
a dizzying transition game. Every player on every
team who ever won the Cup gets to take it home; it
has partied on front lawns, swimming pools and in
the trunks of cars, and even the guy who left it by
the side of the road and drove away, still, he thinks
of it as holy. And that word – *holy* – appears most
in the conversation of veterans who know how the
touch fades, the shoulder takes longer between days
of easy movement, how Bobby Hull passed on his
only chance to drink champagne from its lip when
the Hawks won it '61 because he thought there'd be
so many in his life. Some take the Cup apart, clean
the rings, make minor repairs in their basements
and then inscribe on the inside of the column the
unofficial log of their intimate knowledge: This way
I have loved you.

AT THE HOCKEY HALL OF FAME I SAW

the Russian sweaters from '72: they were homemade
and eccentric – wool with tiny, felt letters sewn on,
the letters curled from the wool, like the bits on the
costumes my mother sewed for the school centennial
pageant where I was a boy transported a hundred
years into the future, to the Canada I'd never see:
smooth-running and prosperous and completely
English, like the school. Above their old clothes,
the players move in ways only skating can offer:
hips extended, heads leaning, the hands forging
a perfect circuit with the stick and the padded
shoulders, legs together to the side, an angle only
speed delivers from falling.

LANGUAGE

This is the season Jagr will blossom: his 3rd as a pro,
2 Stanley Cups, a great playoffs behind him. This year
John Kordic is dead. In my mind I've followed him after
games to the strip bars of Yonge Street where John
bought the line that sex can be made simple as hockey;
in the dark of the Zanzibar he finds his place smoothly,
opens the hands he balled into fists in the Gardens.
He asks the woman to the table to dance; before
she begins, he says, *Don't turn around.* In the pool, we
are gearing up for the draft, the league in flux because
of the European talent. Did you see Jagr score in the
game that eliminated Chicago? Stickhandling around
three men then slipping the puck past Belfour like
a surprise confession. They asked him how he did it,
but he couldn't explain; lacking the language to
describe his own body, he is only more beautiful.

A LIFETIME OF MOVING THE BODY JUST SO

Once I saw Gordie Howe flick a stick full of rink chaff over
the head of a collector looking for autographed pucks at an
old-timers game; Gordie, never taking his eyes off the
guy, sent the snow in a perfect arc from the blade resting on
the ice. Even the guy had to admire his dexterity, a lifetime
of moving the body just so. So he said, *Thank you*, and went
back to his seat. Hockey looks simple and fast the way
sumo looks simple and fast, yet there are 78 named moves
in sumo, though a match is over in 9 seconds or less, the
time it takes a man to score a goal and the two who get
assists to set him up. Its wisdom is briefly spoken, but takes
years to hear. Gordie told the future, *Work on your backhand.*

OPEN TO THE PUBLIC: VISITORS' DRESSING ROOM, MAPLE LEAF GARDENS

*In the autumn of 1992, management invited fans to tour
the building freely for the first time in years.*

Most teams spent the '70s and '80s in here holding
the lead on the Leafs, this tiny room with the missing
hooks replaced by 3-inch nails haphazard from the walls
as if they'd grown there. The high school student
behind me on our tour inhales it deeply through his nose,
throws out his arms to get even more of the sweaty air
into his lungs. *It's a* locker room *all right!* he exhales loud
and happy and 17; it's the weight room at school where
he and his team work out together and for the yearbook
photograph gathered naked behind the weights; they'll
laugh about it when it's printed, and years from now ask,
Where's that guy? . . . And him? . . . Whatever happened to . . . ?
the way men who played for those Leafs look hard at
team pictures for what they might have been had they
only visited this place they spent their short careers as
pro; with a stadium so empty it filled 4 pages in *Sports
Illustrated*, the fans in Minnesota shamed their team's
lousy owners from the rink. With sellout crowds,
Toronto booed Bobby Orr and hung his sweater
on a nail.

ACTS OF WORSHIP

*If you're too much in awe, you'll never love this
game. Sooner or later, you've got to hit Gordie and
flatten him if you can the way Henry Moore used to
have his kids piss on each of his sculptures when
they were done to show they were, after all, only
things. Of course you can't. Gordie is just too strong.
But if you're lucky, he'll give you an elbow behind
the ref's back and you'll see what a bastard he is.
That'll cure you.*

USING THE BODY

It's the instruction for goons, use the body, pound
the other guy rougher than his game imagines, the
body hitting home, the body the agent of policy.
When a fight begins, we say it is emotion, but after
the game, the goon speaks calmly of the momentum
of play, doing what he has to do, a strict account
level in his head. Later, when he wears a suit,
when he coaches, you can see how he saw the
entire rink all along: he never looked at the puck,
the stickhandling, a man's cheek when his purpose
is clear and there's open ice before him. He saw
the solid mass of a man, how the game, flimsy
as a wing, could be held at the socket where
the wing joins the body, and broken.

I WATCH HIM BREAK SANDSTROM'S LEG

and I find myself longing for a big, tough man
with a nickname like "the Hammer" as if an enforcer
with the right rink smarts and the will to go the
distance with anyone on the ice could protect
his friends from the kind of hit that ends a career,
the violence within the rules. Fact is, there is no fight;
fact is, the Kings go down in six. We've just been
through a war – even that is not enough when men
are willing, the outcome is in doubt and the ache
in me is to strike, I who am not hungry, not broken.

DEFENCE MECHANISMS

Because his jaw was broken when he knelt between
the shooter and the open net, he's vanished from the
lineup. Then the commentators say the team is better
off without him, and my anger rises: he gave everything
to that team he carried all year. Yet I catch myself
in the same words about the family I made and left.
We are talking these days about children, and the
bad example I set when I cut an apple, holding it
in my palm, and at last, cut my finger. I, who take
my hands from my pockets when I see a mother
carry her newborn across the threshold of the
subway door in case the baby falls, or the doors
begin to close. I, who once had four names to
offer with my own, and now say they are better
off without me.

LINDROS

has become unavoidable, appears in the NHL's *75th
Anniversary Commemorative Book* though at the time
of printing he hadn't played a minute in the NHL.
Some people make your history from the out-
side like Marx and Russia where they played the team
concept to perfection. When their veterans came over,
the skill they lacked most was taking the shot without
passing, and Makarov led the league without scoring
a goal. Ken Dryden says the famous *soft hands* is
because the Russians were afraid of breaking their
shoddy sticks, but Lindros is afraid of breaking
nothing. In a single game in Maple Leaf Gardens,
I saw him bust a man's collarbone and nearly break
another man's leg, score one goal and assist on another,
and it proves how little we have for ourselves: given the
chance that night, I'd be him.

THE SILENCE OF 17,000

The Forum, December 11, 1989, five days after
the murder of fourteen women in the Montreal Massacre

17,000 who came for noise drawn to silence in their
memory this building the shape of the inside of
the mouth it waits for air the women of École
Polytechnique fill the Forum we swear we will never
forget but words return and we take sides dressed
in language as the men we surround are dressed in
opposing cities we shame and glorify ourselves each
season the enemy goalie wears a white ribbon under
his helmet he shakes his head when the siren sounds
the game begins the police arrive too late:
as many dead as on the ice before us.

RHÉAUME

Here is the desire of Manon Rhéaume: to stop the
puck. Come down from the stands, strap on the big
pads, painted mask, disappear into *goalie* the way
a man can be a man and not a man inside the
armour. To forget in the motion of the save that we
do not forget she is always a woman and sex is
everything: if she wasn't pretty she'd never hear her
looks got her on the NHL team in Tampa Bay
where the ushers are women hired from a bar
called Hooters, and David Letterman wouldn't have
her on *Late Night,* prodding her again and again, *Say
Ock-ee*; if Brett Hull was ugly as a wet owl and
scored 86 goals a season, still there'd be kids with
his poster on their bedroom doors. To be a woman
and have it be her play that counts. To stop the
puck where the best are men, for men to be better
than they are. On your wall is a collage of women
with their arms raised, they are dancing, they are
lifting weights, they are marching against apartheid.
One is a goddess with snakes in her hands,
Catwoman reaches for Gotham, Boadicea shakes a
spear in the face of Rome, two nuns run splashing
into the laughing waves: here, I give you Rhéaume
and a glove save, the puck heading for the top
corner. Stopped.

ALL-STAR ACTION

*January 19, 1991: Desert Storm begins the war on Iraq
three days before the annual All-Star Game*

Even the greatest player in the world asks, *What
are we here for?* and votes to cancel play. But
they don't, just as I am writing this, when the war
has begun, and bombs become the *thousand
points of light* once the bad joke of an American
election. The men shift listlessly on their skates as
a woman whose brother is a pilot in the Gulf sings
the national anthem. The puck is dropped. Later,
I will scan the papers for the numbers that mean
the acts of men. And as they score the surface, we
hear again the scour of metal on ice; the crowd
stares past them, dizzy with fear for the boys they
are so proud of. Below the ice, distant at first, and
moving under the sliding men, they appear: blade-
shaped, graphic the way insects are, the airplanes.
They rise towards the ice from the sky below,
larger now, faster, their steel tails scraping the ice;
they move under the men, imitating them perfectly –
passing, shooting . . . passing, shooting.

COACH'S CORNER

The almost clerical collar, he is the priest of rock 'em
sock 'em. He silences his more knowledgeable friends
with his faith in the bodies of men and without him
and his kind the NHL would be as vapid as the All-Star
Game forever. He is loud and whiny and complaining,
and he chokes up on air if he's hurt by someone's words –
everything a man should not be, yet every sports bar
wills itself to quiet, turns up the volume on its dozen
sets only for his words. He is their man in a way no
hero of the play could be; his big league career was a
single game, but remember, he used to tell Bobby Orr
what to do, and Bobby listened as we listen though
we let the game go on in silence. He slams foreigners,
praises women in all the ways wrong for our time,
rejects any wavering in the masculinity of his troops
like a colonel in the US Marines. And yet he is here
because he is unafraid to love, love the game, the
journeyman players, love the code that makes a man
a man – and if you don't know it I ain't gonna tell ya.
He loves the fans, for all the pain we cause him, and
we are here with our own uncomfortable backs for that
dogged love, the voice that rises like a tenor sax, the
pointed finger, eyes narrowed to divine the world
that's got him trapped on two sides already.

ZAMBONI

Zamboni has come! Rejoice!
That which is old shall be made new –
and right before your eyes, to boot –
in scalding water, a spinning brush
and a Celtic love knot's route
around the rink at a pace that says, *There is no rush.*
The stage is flat, and everything worth watching
will happen where Zamboni spreads the world
to all four corners of its map. Arena tractor, boxy
as a child's drawing of a truck, it breaks the game
to make more game, and then departs by its
circus-elephant door. And there it is: before
the players take the competitive ice again,
the moment, serene in neither victory nor loss,
the time between the answer and its prayer.

TWO POEMS FOR EMMA, AGE ONE

1. Public Skating at the Olympic Oval

After 3 years' absence, I'm back
on the rink. Right now, you are too young to
appreciate the irony of steel between
me and a Herculean pond where I forget
everything I ever knew how to do on skates – yes,
I lost all my body once possessed of soaring
a circular breeze among schoolchildren turning
and turning the untiring gyre of a truly Canadian
O. Ms. Harrison Rouleau,
for the part of you from Britain and France, the part
to which we are supposed to bend in literature and speech,
this ice is the perishing of the world.
But here, where knees are bent on a frozen lake
to give power to the moving figure, this ice teaches, this ice
is the birth of play. Here are my hands. You reach up,
grab them and run the only way you know: head forward,
torso like a skater's at the angle of falling,
working the carpet like a pair of foot pumps;
you are getting ready for this abandon, this disproportion,
and I, learning how not to think
of my body again and just go and go,
I remember.

2. Ice

The puck is dropped. Naming begins: *This is a puck.*
Puh, she replies; *puh*, she whispers.
There are only so many apologies,
                    so many startings over.

This is one, a baby at thirteen months saying, *puh*,
holding the flat, hard face to her face, her breath
sketching itself in the winter air against the new moon
                    in her mittened hand.

After confession and prayer, the slate is wiped clean
for the truly repentant. This is how I understand it,
how it is mocked by the lie and faith
                    reasoned in a circle.

The puck participates in both the sphere and the cube.
I slide it down the grey sheet of ice like a curler with
first rock. On this ice, I can teach something
                    about force and motion.

Puh, she says, and points. *Let's go get it,* I say. *Let's go!*
Every year the ice – new like the fresh page, conception,
birth, a life converted mid-sentence – we say,
                    has seen the light.

If the Earth were just that bit further from the sun
(say the planet was a human head, I mean
the length a hair grows overnight) it would be
winter everywhere, and Christ in buried Jerusalem
                    would have said,

This is the water upon which I build my church.

FACE-OFF

They lean forward, sticks extended, faces poised almost,
from my angle, as if to kiss as they kissed in the NBA
finals: Isiah Thomas and Magic Johnson: the name of
a prophet, the faith of a wizard. Can we hope for such
reconciliation? Hallowe'en at last a memorial for 300
years of women burning for their knowledge at the
pyres of the Church, men, crowded around their good
good work, their faces implacable even with the
screaming in their ears; for men to kiss while thousands
cheer them? Or is it only here, the imagined ground,
where faces are not masks, are not brought bare
into each other's view only to dare each other –
Take this off if you can.

ALL-TIME GAME

One-on-one we are drafting the all-time game
between us, my brother and I. Not the Official
All-Time Team of Six with no one to play, we are
truly opposed, the language inflated and gross the
way men talk when they mean it pretending they don't.
The Big Six are all English, which I say reflects
the voters. Then I say I could beat those guys
with Lemieux, Robitaille and the Rocket up front,
Bourque and Savard on the blue line, Plante in net.
He says we should draft for the ultimate game,
and the heavy checkers come out of our mouths,
the *policemen*, and our finesse players get banged up
along the boards. The game deteriorates; because
he nearly killed a man, I pick Eddie Shore. It's like
this over table hockey, us at each other, huge pucks
in the tiny nets, the anger of 30 years, everything
out of proportion.

THE USE OF FORCE

New York Rangers at Montreal, February 9, 1991

It boils at the centre of the game: Lyle, the home team
boy, pulling Randy, from New York, away from the
clot of men in the corner of the rink. Lyle wants to
fight, and Randy, the smaller man, holds big Lyle's jersey
at the cuffs, trying to pin his arms. Gently, almost like
leaves on a stream, they drift towards centre, their
hands naked now, their heads unhelmeted; this is the
undressing. Soon we'll see them pull at each other's
sweaters, we'll see the padding each man has strapped
around his chest, the body covered in fragments: a
piece . . . a space . . . a piece. . . . But then Lyle's hand
pops free and his bared fist goes down and down on
Randy's face, and the crowd's anticipation, the listless,
frustrating play of the home team, bursts from the
throats of the 17,000 at the Forum that night, a roar
I can feel tremble down the centre of my rib cage, my
stomach, my groin, the way Polynesian sailors without
compasses navigated their reedy boats, their genitals
feeling the roll of the sea (and I'm in Canada in a huge,
cold room). Lyle has finished his offering to the crowd,
and the officials draw lines between him and the
shaking Randy; I can still hear my parents saying, when
I saw my first hockey fight on TV, *They can't punch very
hard on skates.* But Randy has been brought to the ice,
his sky filled with Lyle's fist, and the Rangers do not
fare well this night, while the Canadiens find Caesar's
tide, and break the game open in their favour.

BERTUZZI

There was a time everyone was terrified of him, the way
everyone is terrified of bears, but still, before television,
hundreds of years of English fun were had in chaining one
up and summoning the village for an afternoon of baiting
and fire. Bertuzzi, the big body out there, putting the weight
in an equation his opponents had been trying to unbalance
his whole career. In *Sports Illustrated*, defencemen bragged
they knew how to push their lips close to the crease of his
ear and say the words that threw all 245 pounds of him off
his game. Safe behind arena glass, fans called him out with
placards announcing He Wore Pink Underwear. And then
some radio jock mouthed off about doing his wife.
Everyone asks for analysis, condemnation, a trial; they pore
over his history in the Sault when he chased an entire team
through the parking lot and kept after them even after their
bus pulled out, shouting and banging his stick against the
windows. Every act of violence is the last in a complicated
play, and the Greeks, who made a science of such emotions
and how to coach them, called this one *Até*, the rage that
seems nothing but its own object, the fuel a man must light
for what he must do in war, even to the weak and small, the
moment a fist is made heavy not by blood and muscle, but
ridiculed manhood, eyeballed wife, fallen friend, his power
to gather everything a life could ever be and throw it down
without a second thought.

NH ELEGY FOR THE LOCKOUT YEAR

(September 2004–July 2005)

Once, men came home from war,
or from the sides of family graves,
to lace up skates and play for the Cup
as if everything could be remade
in a silver bowl passed hand to hand.
For years it etched the seasons
with their winning names,
and took the touch of triumph
into each triumphant house. One year
it paused to mourn the dead, and
stayed unmarked to mark their passing.
Today, left idle in the Hall of Fame,
while rich men quarrel to no profit at its base,
untouched upon its plinth it stands.
And all who see it can tell you now
a fallen thing is one that no one holds.

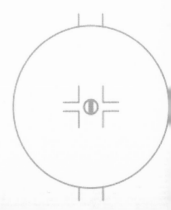

PENALTY

This was the day Nelson Mandela came to say
thank you to West Africa, the day Nelson and
the dictator of Ghana were driven through the city
streets in an open truck. A people's day, the way
cleared by troops looking for assassins, seeing them
everywhere – Mandela was coming! The crowd I
was in surged forward, breaking the plane of the
curb like a goal line. The soldiers stopped. The crowd
booed. And a certain soldier got out of his jeep,
glaring. A woman whispered, *Leave,* but I stood,
the way a fan stands at the glass for the action
on the other side. And down came his boot –
BOOM! And the crowd spun round, pivoting
in their sandals, and they ran and knocked me
down so I lay in the street with all their sandals
like gloves on the ice after a bench brawl.

SHRINE

Surrounded by the dead, the cool stone walls of
the dead, the stain of glass backlit by the African sun
blazing with the faces of the vividly departed –
age 31; age 34, the age at which now, here, a man
hangs up his skates and goes into business or
coaching. On the cards, the high-speed film traps
Béliveau and Hull mid-flight. When a generation's
work is done by 35, by the time you're 35, you've
seen four generations. I remember Keon and
Armstrong of the last great Leafs; Espo and Orr and
Boston; I remember Lafleur and I remember
the Islanders. I remember Gretzky entering the game.
Imagine a life the span a career is now, how it must
be to grow old, polish the names you knew as
a child so they would not be forgotten, the way
names are forgotten to all but collectors of plaques
and cards, names entwined in your memory with light.

BÉLIVEAU TEACHES ME HOW TO HANDLE THE PUCK

We used to have breakfast together in the '60s; me with
a bowl and milk and my early reading eyes, him on the back
of a box of Shredded Wheat – it's the tall picture of him,
the one that hangs in the Forum, Béliveau coming straight
at you surrounded by a stadium in darkness, and even
though the ice is flat, he always looks as if he's coming over
the horizon like a mast: Béliveau skating the edge between
old world and new, Béliveau in charge the way the eye of a
hurricane is in charge. He teaches me not to look at the
whirl of legs and arms and wood, or be impressed by the
thunder of the puck striking the boards, filling the ear of the
arena. He teaches me, *The puck going into the net is silent.*

MAURICE

I've been rinkside while veteran players banged the ice like the edges of a sealskin drum in his name. Who hasn't seen the picture of him going in on goal with his eyes ablaze and bituminous black? Or been given his measure with the story of the 160-pound Richard dragging Earl Seibert, a 225-pound defenceman who hung onto his sweater, all the way from the upper circle to the best seat in the house to watch him score? The story I want to tell you is this: against the weight of disease and his doctor's advice not to travel, when he was asked to send an autographed jersey to our town instead, he said in words what he told Earl with his shoulders way back then, *Forget the sweater, I'm coming.*

MY FATHER'S FACE

To begin (always beginning) to speak of my father's
face uncovered at last – Coffey's determined look
up ice, Messier's gaze which weighs 200 pounds, the
faces of the village elders in Ghana who are their
world's law and I stared into through a camera, my
only permission to look so long – I look away and
down; the eyes of the player captured on film
beating another for the sports page, a red glove
breaks a jaw (the man plays with emotion); my
father as a boy, his face in a grip between the thumb
and index of *his* father's hand, my grandfather
saying, *A small face, big as a twopenny ball,* my father
disgraced by a story a lifetime old – he picks a
squash ball up, and it reminds him, the words work
his jaw like his favourite poems, the language
excessive with meaning; there, within the eyes of the
soldier who made the crowd round me run from his
stamped foot so fast they left their shoes in the
street, the face that could shoot; that face, advancing
on me over a fight at dinner: for backing down
from that face, myself I have praised and been
praised for the peace. I have made so much peace
backing down. Shot along the boards of a perfect
rink, the puck describes the universe and returns,
that face I show you in anger my own.

THIS IS MY HOCKEY

Hello, Dad. This is my hockey. Did you ever see me play it? I dream you in the stands, no longer running. You appear in my words as if years ago you died and made absence your only fault. This is the lie that keeps us looking in the faces of worshipped men: if only you were there, then everything would have been OK, everything would have been good. Really, you are perfect, perfect in the fearful story, perfect in the highlight film, perfect as you limp from the ice between your teammates, the iron box of your face unhinged *oh no oh no* going through your mind as you cannot put your weight down; you are perfect in your demonstration of the triple jump that won you the championship of the army games in Asia; perfect again in your every word, your son is not a strong boy, your allergic son who breathes whistling in the sick spring air.

TIE GAME

For the team

A good game repairs the boy inside me – I mean a *good*
game as spoken of in the language of men. Everyone
knows – win or lose – you did what was asked, the guy
with the puck counted on you in position whether he
passed or not, and the one that rang off the post was still
hailed as a good shot in words heard round the rink;
when the better shooter says, *Take it!* This is impersonal
love, this movement of men on the ice, thinking, talking
all the time, playing the angles and each other, the love
the mind has for the body, the key for the lock, the one
for machines that always started in the cold. Today,
because of how we felt, we let the game end in a tie.
You don't see that every day, but one of us was leaving
town next week, and we couldn't let him go with that
good game dying in victory or defeat.

THE HERO IN OVERTIME

For Eric Marsden, June 20, 1999

is Brett Hull at 54:41 of OT, game 6 in Buffalo, shoving
the puck past Hasek who's fallen to the ice, as he usually
does, flat as bread. Now he's toast, and the Sabres, too:
it's over and over in the way of all finals. In the Dallas
dressing room, they're bearing the Cup full of spinning
champagne. And the magic of the microphone in Bob-
the-Commentator's hands reveals the giddy boy in each
hardened ice warrior thanking Mom and Dad and all his
friends – by name – from the little town of his birth
on national TV. In the smallest hours of Father's Day,
my daughter and Eric's daughters are asleep in the upper
storeys of the house where their dads are whooping it up
on the ground floor below. Later the girls will wake us
with their cards and their hand-painted gifts and their as
yet unalloyed love. But it's not too early for our man Bob
to bring Brett to the screen to remind him yet again he's
from a great hockey family, and confess who he was
thinking of when he scored the biggest tally of his life.
But the microphone can't remake Brett. Brett believes in
words over the body, in what you do over who you were
born to. Despite all the prompting towards the lore of his
mighty father, whose carved name glistens from the
wetted silver surface in the halogen gaze of the camera,
it's words Brett was thinking of in the fold before the
net – derogatory words shot at his goalie who, it was
said, couldn't win the big one, his teammates who
would never be complete without this moment they'd
never have. Then he turns his mind to the Cup, the
pedestal that's a statue to itself; he reaches for a way to
make words come from it to answer everything in the air
the way it does in his chest. He smiles – there are no
words for this. But he has done what no other player has done
tonight – he thanked his children, whom I've
forgotten, who the viewers will never know unless they,
someday, too, bulge the twine for the team. *I'd like to
thank my kids*, he says, who he sees at the top of his dreams.

ODE TO THE SADDLEDOME

It looks like the Ark. And that makes sense – the game
is also a species that needs two sides to survive. If
Genesis had been set in the sunny badlands of Alberta,
there it would be on the ocean of God's disappointment:
the big boat, a sheet of ice in its belly, and a 40-day
playoff to settle it once and for all. I remember the night
we took Louis de Bernières to the Dome for the Flames'
opening round tilt against the Hawks. It was his first
game, and it ran into triple overtime. It ended in a bad
bounce, the way all things end that must because the
body weakens, and *puck* is the Devil's most endearing
name. I apologized to Louis for the endlessness of play.
It's all right, he said, *I'm English. I watch cricket.* The Dome
gathered me in when I first arrived, reading my poems to
the echo of hockey below deck – voices calling out from
the rink, the wooden report of passes and shots under a
roof the shape of a giant ear. I fancy that the building
actually hears us, and the spectators, famously quiet in
Calgary, take the cue and come to listen. The best sound
in the game, they'll tell you, is made when all else is silent
and the skater's blade etches into frozen water the path of
a sharp bank, the ice turned to steam around silver. The
Stanley Cup was paraded in this place. Olympians went
head-to-head in a beauty fierce as plumage; people who
never raise their voices love openly, or hate, and when the
conflict subsides, and the tall doors open to the
surrounding land, we all walk down the mountain
side by side with a story.

THE PHANTOM GOAL

Even after all that followed, it's still a thing of beauty,
that puck angled up just right off Gelinas' skate towards
the net where the great goal scorers go, meeting
Khabibulin's sweeping pad that smacks it back into
the play at just the speed to split the second where
In meets Out; Cup-Winning Goal, Elimination Saving
Save; Cup Champion and Runner-Up. A spinning coin
is heads and tails at once. Everything in the game of
hockey that happens or doesn't, happened right then,
the moment a man's armoured leg met a circle the size of
his palm at top speed over a line of paint embedded in
the ice with the same astonishing precision it would take
to swat a fly out of the air with a two-by-four. There are
many here who'll tell you he didn't do it; the puck was in,
the game was ours, and the refs missed the cause of an
immortal joy ten thousand eyes beheld. And the game
went on, and Tampa won, and won again, and lofted the
Cup in the Florida sun where it shone like phosphorus on
fire. The Flames gathered their Mile of fans all dressed in
red in the city square, and promised us next time they'd
bring home the Cup themselves. They never did, not even
close, and no one is left to ice from that old team. The League
told the League's own Chairman of the Board they ran
the tapes and the puck was only three-quarters of the way
across, but it's too late for proof – they'll tell you here
they should have stopped and checked it instead of letting
the Lightning go back down the rink and score. It doesn't
take much to bring the conversation back to what we lost
when that puck was all and nothing at once, and here's
where sport is different from what we're taught; if it's
truly love you have for the team, it's also a wound
forever.

NOW IS THE WINTER

With the last ounces of his grace, my father
stands up from his wheelchair, turns toward
the bed as though the floor is ice;
he tilts his spine, knees bent, and waits to shift
his weight to mine; I lay him on the blanket
and kiss his lips. We talk of Shakespeare
who carried him line by line through tropic wars
to the final surgery on his failing hips.
Now is the winter of our discontent,
he recites from those pages of his brain
no disease has yet erased,
the words the prayer of one
who has no god to hear his cries, his powers spent.
When he asks, I promise to be with him when he dies,
and winter stirs in the broken fingers
of my hand that long ago healed winter cold
into mended bone. My father sleeps as the land sleeps –
and I am taught that nothing is immortal
and awake forever. Outside, the heroes, green,
and knowing only what they see,
take their sticks and pucks and
lean into their shots
while the mid-winter's night
dreams water turned to stone beneath their feet.

THE FEMININE REDUX

My choir sang "O Canada" at the women's finals at Olympic Park in 2017. A lot of things are true that weren't before, starting with me, singing. Let me deal you from a deck of hockey tarot cards. Here's the Trainer Running to the Fallen Man Beside the Boards. That's me on the ice, and I can't tell you how many times since we last talked about women and men and whether there would ever be a card called simply the Player, but I saw Canada's women's team take gold in Buffalo four years ago, and the arena was full-voiced with fans. So were the bars, the Americans cheering for the States, Canada cheering for Canada, and I have seen the day it didn't matter, woman or man, they were just the Players, and it was beautiful. Here's the Hall of Fame, and here's the Analyst working the men's game for *Hockey Night*. We know the rarity of things two ways: first when they don't happen as much as they used to, and second, when it's been too long since they happened before. I know my history: with women's hockey, it's been both. There's the Ice, the Mask, the Puck; in their indifference to sex, they say the game belongs to those who want it, end of story. Here are the stands that demand we sit and love it all. Here's the future. Take your seat beside me. There is still much to do, but the anthem is over and, tonight, the women have a game to play.

ELEGY FOR THE ROCKET

For a minute or two, I spoke with him, Maurice Richard,
the month before he died. He told me his legs *were gone*
from the medicine; the room was crowded and hot.
I brought him water and dared that moment to look
right into those famous eyes so dark with their official
colour they looked pure pupil. We've all heard men say
they were afire like coal, and maybe it was that language
that affected me because what came to mind as I
considered the grey lace woven where the iris is lined
with muscle was the way briquettes burn out under the
grill – such a small image, I know. And in the tranquil
now I can conjure charred wood veined with burnt-out
embers, or the remains of a home set ablaze rather than
surrendered out of *War and Peace* – a book worthy of
the public stature of the man – but the truth is, up close,
not staring me down to score a goal, those eyes were
a humble fire at the end of its use. And all the ferocity
of the man and his reputation couldn't hide in his fading
light what they also knew who lined up by the thousand
round the Forum to say farewell, and wept on all the
streets ringing Notre-Dame at his passing.

THE VIEW FROM THE TOP

Every player on every team who ever won the Cup gets to take it home.
— Stanley Cup

And at the top of Mount Fisher, 9000 feet up in the
Rockies, Scott Niedermayer lifts the Stanley Cup above
his head. The New Jersey defenceman's wearing red, the
Devils' colour at home, and he's balanced on a slab no
bigger than a goal crease over Cranbrook, BC, where he
was raised, and he grips the rims of the trophy as if it
holds him to a point in the stony crown of the whole
wide world; I tell you, no jar on a hill in Tennessee ever
stopped time and stuffed all the eye can behold into the
barrel of itself better than this Cup at the summit of
Niedermayer's arms. What the photographer,
helicoptered to the peak behind him, and not far
removed, cannot catch on film is his face, the look
between a hockey man and his gods exchanged over the
giants who slouch their shoulders round the valley where
he first set his steel on water frozen calm.

58 SECONDS

Like all of you, I'm proud to call Las Vegas home. I met my wife here, my kids were born here, and I know how special this city is. To all the brave first responders that have worked timelessly and courageously throughout this whole tragedy, we thank you. To the families and friends of the victims, know that we'll do everything we can to help you and our city heal. We are Vegas strong.

– Deryk Engelland, Vegas Golden Knights Opening Night,
October 10, 2017

This is not a poem I started in search of something in
the language beneath the keyboard like the ocean under a
pier. This is to remember with you this speech from a
week after the shootings in Las Vegas killed 58 at a
concert within range of a broken window at the Mandalay
Bay hotel. It took Deryk 58 seconds to say it at centre ice
in the arena where the multitudes came to be contained,
the way they still come to Vegas, meaning the gunman
lost his war. There is nothing more immortal than words.
They have outlasted the gods and terrors and they are still
here, holding us as we hold on. Hockey's greatest political
victory was the '72 Summit Series because we got shocked into
respect for the way the Soviets played the game, and
ordinary Russians saw Westerners for the first time, and
saw we were not monsters, though clearly the monstrous
walk among us every day. Hockey's victory is diplomatic,
which is to say, we are all in this together. Deryk's speech
was one such beginning, and Deryk scored a goal right
after that, and the Golden Knights played out of their
minds that year. If you want a reason for sport, it's that
season, when the body answered death with the pageantry
of bodies in motion that made its poetry true.

HUSH

Sshhhh, sshhhh, the skater stops, *husshhhh,* turning
sideways to the flow of the body, the ice.
Hush, my beloved son, in whom I am well pleased;
this painful land smiles inside the leper in the
street; her extended hand – you take it, *sshhhh,* no
one is here who has ever done you harm, no one;
you might die in this land, which is to say you
might die here, and the strange place makes what
you have always known clear to you – *What
would you have left undone?* The sound of ice,
the puck cradled in the stick, the skater turns *sshhhh,*
the bath is drawn, warm water, my huge hand;
you have found me out.

SADDLEDOME: AFTER THE FLOOD

This is the Ark after the Flood:
>hull full of water, the animals gone.

I feel more for Noah after this,
>getting drunk every night since dry land
>>knowing *dry land* as a faith
>>>that would never return.

Water is complicated:
>see how brown in these pictures it is,
>>how full of the earth it leaves behind
>when the river packs up and heads back to bed.

That's microbial brown,
>>fertility,
>>>earthworm realm,
>the colour of the soil
>>that binds with naked feet.

●

I've loved the parabola in its roof,
>the Saddledome: I'll miss it when they
>>build the next entertainment colossus

and the game is something someone is doing in one room
>while the television is on in another.

Remember the days
when everyone gathered around the set to eat
>because anything on it was only on then?

The Saddledome remembers,
and those days were not so long ago,
>though they became far, far away in a flash
>>like the time you
>>>dropped your car keys down the sewer.

After the flood, I saw a lovely 42-inch television
       sitting on a dolly outside someone's home,
            and I thought,
          even if that TV was brand new,
              what I want to steal is the dolly.

After the flood,
     my basement
     was the Event Level of the Saddledome,
water up to the expensive seats,
     shelves full of the books I read
     while I was finding my writing voice,
       boxes of archives
           in torrential disarray.

I feel for the Dome.

I feel for Theo Fleury
     hurling himself like
a takeout-weight curling stone the length of the ice,
       arms pumping in a hockey joy so great
          he forgot for a moment his
     suicidally crippling secrets –

What I want is that joy in the poem.
     The best lines from 30 years of
       paper tossed afloat
          are the ones I dismissed
     or misread when I saw them.

Consider:
Sometime in the early 1980s I handwrote,

Is this art
that I have mastered it so quickly?

When I took it from the blur of water,
I read it out loud and said instead,

Is this art, that I have misunderstood it so soon?
   and it became a line for a poem at last.

Poetry is play, even in the darkest of its discontents.
Poetry is a sex abuse victim,
   shoulders back, roaring out the body alive,
and rhyme is the laughter of disasters we survive.

That's why the hockey book was the door for me
from saying to writing,
   from myself to the poem,
from me to you.

That's why.

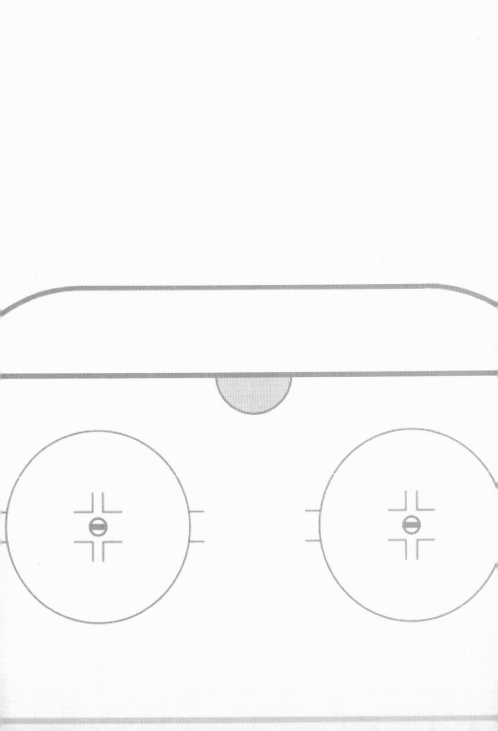

NOTES AND ACKNOWLEDGEMENTS

Poems from *Hero of the Play*

Unless otherwise noted below, the poems here are either reprinted from *Hero of the Play* or from *Hero of the Play: 10th Anniversary Edition*, both from Wolsak and Wynn, 1994 and 2004 respectively, or they are versions of those poems I have revised over the years and which appear for the first time in this book.

Poems from Other Books

"Why the Peterborough Petes Won the Memorial Cup" originally appeared in *Fathers Never Leave You* (Mosaic Press, 1987); it has been revised for this edition.

"Two Poems for Emma, Age One: 1. Public Skating at the Olympic Oval; and 2. Ice" originally appeared in *Big Breath of a Wish* (Wolsak and Wynn, 1998).

"Now is the Winter" originally appeared in *On Not Losing My Father's Ashes in the Flood* (Wolsak & Wynn, 2016).

"Saddledome: After the Flood" also originally appeared in *On Not Losing My Father's Ashes in the Flood.* For the record, the "Entertainment Colossus" it speaks of was approved by Calgary City Council on July 30, 2019. The Saddledome is scheduled to be demolished in 2024.

Poems Published Here for the First Time in Book Form

"Resting Places"

"A Mid-Ice Proposal"

"Zamboni"

"Bertuzzi." Note, this poem refers to the Todd Bertuzzi/Steve Moore incident of March 8, 2004. The protagonist in this poem is not to be confused with the Bertuzzi currently playing in the NHL.

"NH Elegy for the Lock-out Year." This poem originally appeared online, on the website for ABEBooks in 1994.

"The Phantom Goal"

"58 Seconds"

"The Feminine Redux"

Poems in this collection have also appeared in the journals *Canadian Literature, Geist, Whetstone, PRISM international, Index, Canada Poetry Review* and *Poetry Toronto*.

They have also been republished in the anthologies *Forward Lines* (forthcoming); *150+: Canada's History in Poetry; The Calgary Project: A City Map in Verse and Visual; The Echoing Years: An Anthology of Poetry from Canada and Ireland; Going Top Shelf: An Anthology of Canadian Hockey Poetry; Echoes 12: Fiction, Media, and Non-Fiction; TransLit: Volume 5* (in French); *Ice: New Writing on Hockey; Poetry Nation: The North American Anthology of Fusion Poetry; Siolence: Poets on Women, Violence, and Silence; Through the Smoky End Boards: Canadian Poetry about Sports and Games; That Sign of Perfection: From Bandy Legs to Beer Legs: Poems and Stories on the Game of Hockey*; and *A Discord of Flags: Canadian Poets Write about the Persian Gulf War*.

A selection of these poems were also performed for *Adrienne Clarkson Presents*.

Recordings of "Resting Places," "African Hockey Poem #1," "Stanley Cup," "Rhéaume" and "Elegy for the Rocket" read by the author are available on the website of *The Poetry Archive* (UK) at www.poetryarchive.org/poet/richard-harrison.

Thank you to my brother Anthony Harrison for creating the original sketches that inspired the book cover.

RICHARD HARRISON is the author of six books of poetry including *On Not Losing My Father's Ashes in the Flood*, which won the Governor General's Award for English-language Poetry and the Stephan G. Stephansson Award for Poetry in Alberta. *25: Hockey Poems, New and Revised* celebrates the twenty-fifth anniversary of the publication of *Hero of the Play*, the first book of poetry to be launched at the Hockey Hall of Fame. Richard's poems have been translated into French, Spanish, Portuguese and Arabic, and his Governor General's Award–winning volume was translated into Italian. He has read widely in Canada and the United States, and his work has been featured on many TV and radio broadcasts including *Adrienne Clarkson Presents* and Peter Gzowski's *Morningside*. His essays, as well as writing on his work, have appeared in several academic publications, the *Globe and Mail*, the *Manchester Guardian* and the *New York Times*. In 1995, Richard was the Distinguished Writer in Residence at the University of Calgary; he has since made Calgary his home and teaches English and Creative Writing at Mount Royal University.

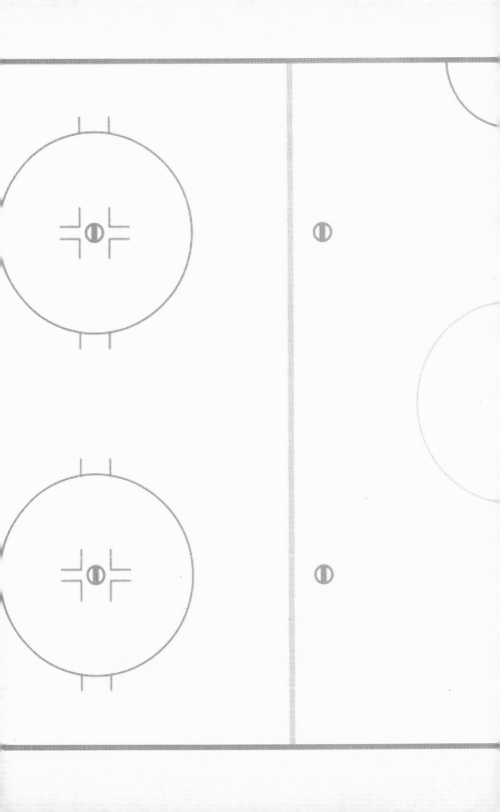

HERO OF THE PLAY

POEMS BY RICHARD HARRISON

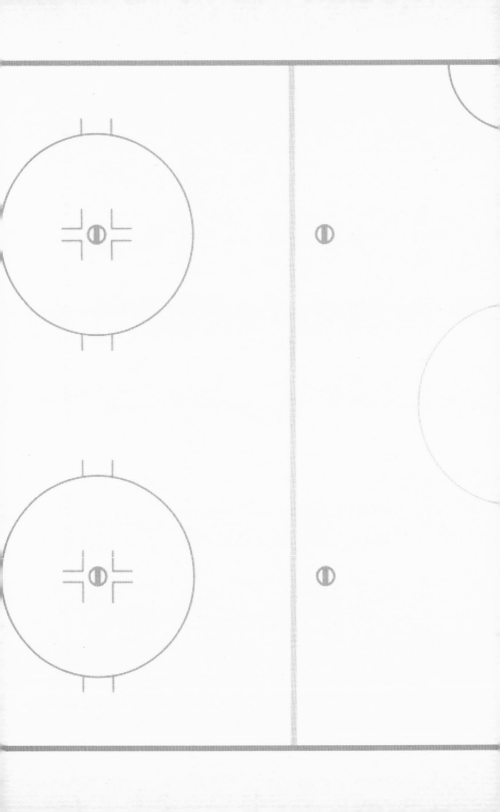

HERO OF THE PLAY

RICHARD HARRISON
Poems revised and New
Foreword by Roy MacGregor

10TH ANNIVERSARY EDITION